Finding Our Way

Written by Robert Roe and Joshua Hatch
Series Consultant: Linda Hoyt

WorldWise™
Content-based Learning

Contents

Introduction

As you finish your maths homework, a clap of thunder shakes your house. Lightning bolts streak across the sky. All the lights in your house turn black – the power has gone out.

You can't see your maths book. You can't even see your hands. All you can see is darkness. All you can hear is rain hitting the roof. You are in your bedroom and you know that the rest of the family is in the living room – you really want to be with them. How will you find your way in the dark?

Even though you can't see, you know where to go. How? You are using your memory.

Chapter 1
Memory maps

In your head, you have a number of memory maps – memories of spaces and places. Memory maps aren't like other maps. Memory maps exist only in your mind. People create them all the time.

Living room

You have a memory map of your room. In the dark, you get up from your chair and reach out your hands. You feel for the wall and take small steps. You don't want to stub your toe on your bed – that would hurt. Your memory map tells you the door of your room is a metre to the left. You take a few steps, hold out your hands and feel for the door. You step into the hallway.

You have a memory map of the whole house. In your mind, you can see the hallway with doors leading to two more bedrooms. At the end of the hallway is the living room. As you shuffle down the hall, you run your hands along the wall. You think to yourself, "The living room should be right about here."

Suddenly, the power comes back on. The hallway fills with light. Just as you thought, you are standing right next to the living room.

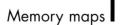

Making a memory map

How many memory maps do you have in your head? Can you **visualise** the **route** you take to get to school? Do you know how to get to school or to your grandparents' house? Think about all the **landmarks** along the way that help you remember how to get to these places.

Draw a map of how you find your way to one of your favourite places – maybe the park, the shopping centre, or a friend's house. What does your memory map look like?

Two people can each have memory maps of the same area, but their memory maps won't be the same.

Get together with a friend from school and have each of you draw a map of your school from memory. Compare the maps you have drawn. How similar are they? They are probably alike in a lot of ways, but they will be different, too.

The reason the maps you have each drawn are different is because you and your friend have different experiences and memories, and those change how your memory maps look. If you really like basketball, you might have drawn that space bigger. If your friend really likes art, he or she might have more detail about the art room.

Chapter 2

Finding your way with a map

When you go somewhere you haven't been before, you need a map. A map is a drawing that shows where things are. Many maps are printed on paper that you can carry with you.

When you go to the zoo, you might be given a paper map showing where everything at the zoo is located. Zoos are big places, and sometimes it can be difficult to find your way around. A map of the zoo will show the different locations of all the animals, and where the cafe and the toilets are located. Using a map makes it easy to find what you're looking for.

Think about ...
What other sort of maps do you use? Do you go hiking? Are there other places you go where you need a map?

The first maps

People have been making maps for thousands of years. Some very old maps show the locations of mountains, rivers and animals to hunt. A long time ago, maps were carved into bones or painted on walls and were definitely not as **convenient** as paper!

Finding your way at sea

The ocean is **vast**, and most often there are no **landmarks** to remember where you have been, or where you are going. So how did early sailors find their way at sea?

One way was to follow the coastline. By keeping land in sight, sailors could easily track where they were going. But staying close to shore is dangerous because underwater rocks and **reefs** can rip holes in boat **hulls**, and many ships are wrecked along rocky coastlines.

To help guide sailors, mapmakers drew detailed maps of the coasts. Every island, **peninsula**, inlet and bay was carefully drawn.

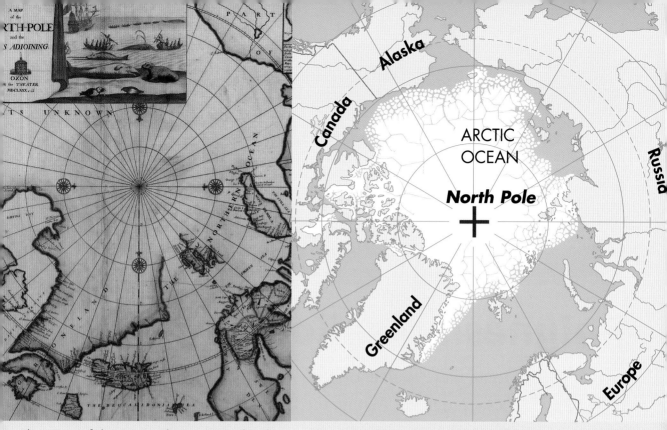

This map of the Arctic shows Greenland and islands that don't exist. It's not even clear where Greenland ends and the "Northern Ocean" begins. At the top, the mapmaker gives up and writes "parts unknown".

This map shows Greenland and the coastline surrounding the Arctic Ocean.

But mapmakers could draw only what they knew, and many had no idea what the world looked like because it had not been mapped. Mapmakers guessed what the coastlines looked like, and some of the guesses look very strange to us now.

Maps aren't very helpful where you can't see land, so what could sailors use when all they could see was water? One group of people came up with some smart solutions.

Chapter 3

Finding your way without a map

Polynesian sailors

In the Pacific Ocean there is an enormous region called the Polynesian triangle. Within the Polynesian triangle there are more than 1,000 small islands. The triangle connects Hawaii, New Zealand and Easter Island, and covers more than 300,000 square kilometres. Often, all you can see is ocean and sky.

The people who lived there 3,500 years ago are known as Polynesians. They are famous for their **seafaring** skills and **intricate** knowledge of sea navigation, which they have passed down through **oral history** from generation to generation. They are believed to be the first group of people to **navigate** the open ocean.

Did you know?

Polynesian sailors relied heavily on their senses, which they used as navigational tools. If Polynesian sailors saw birds in the morning, they knew they were leaving land; if they saw birds in the evening, they knew they were approaching land.

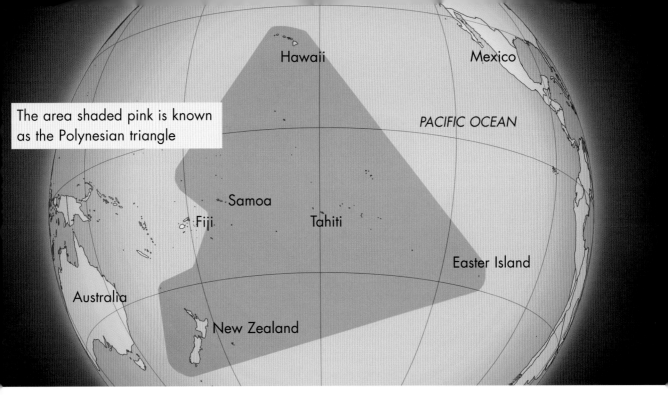

The area shaded pink is known as the Polynesian triangle

Hawaii

Mexico

PACIFIC OCEAN

Samoa

Fiji

Tahiti

Easter Island

Australia

New Zealand

The Polynesians travelled around this region without ever referring to a physical map or using any navigation tools. They travelled by boat from one island to another, even though they couldn't see the islands towards which they were going. They travelled in canoes that could carry people, food and animals.

The Polynesians paid attention to everything around them. By observing every detail, they could work out where they needed to go, and they didn't need to see the land to know where it was.

Question: How could the Polynesians tell where they were going when all they could see was water and sky?

Answer: They saw more than just water and sky. They observed the things around them to help them find their way.

To help find their way, Polynesians observed:
- the stars
- ocean currents and swells
- wind and cloud patterns
- the sun
- colours of the sea and sky
- the weather
- the seasons
- migrating animals such as birds.

Wayfinding

To find their way at sea, Polynesians used the position of the sun during the day, and the position of the moon and stars during the night. They also watched birds, clouds, winds and ocean swells. This technique is called wayfinding.

Polynesians created a map of stars called a **star compass**. They kept track of where and when different stars set so they could figure out where they were just by looking at the night sky.

Wayfinding is part of Polynesian culture. Parents teach their children, and the skills have been passed down from generation to generation.

 Did you know?

Polynesian canoes were around 15 metres long and could carry more than 20 people.

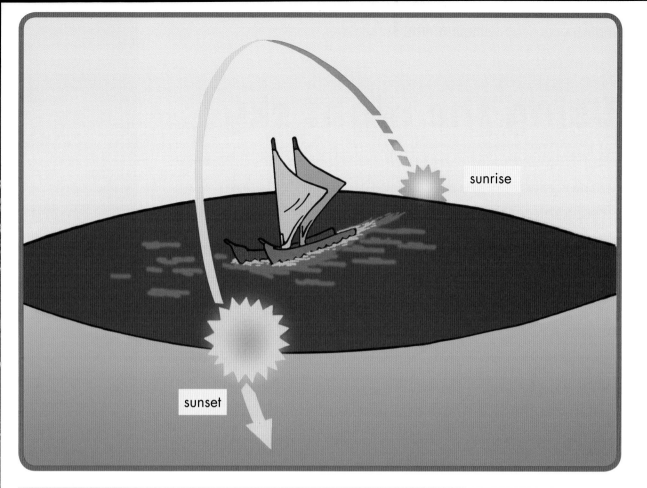

sunrise

sunset

 Did you know?

It's easy to use the sun to determine east and west because the sun always rises in the east and sets in the west. From looking at the sun, you can tell what direction you're facing, but not where you are. To know your location, you need more information.

Using the night sky

People all over the world realised the stars could be used for navigation. That's because the night sky follows a predictable pattern.

In the Southern Hemisphere, you can use the stars of the Southern Cross to find south. Look at the diagram below. Imagine a line across the two stars that make the long axis of the cross. Extend that line across the sky. Now imagine a line connecting the two pointer stars. In the middle of that line, imagine another, at a right angle. Where this line meets the first line is due south. Even though the Southern Cross moves around the sky, drawing those lines will always point you south.

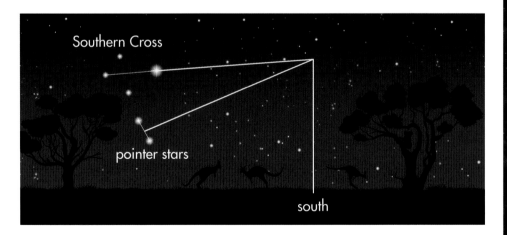

In the **Northern Hemisphere**, one star, Polaris, sits almost directly over the North Pole. All the other stars appear to travel in a circle around it. In reality, all the stars are **stationary**. The earth is turning under Polaris. But if you can find Polaris, then you can find north.

Polaris is known as the North Star.

Sailors measure the horizon, the sun, the moon and various stars. They make this measurement with an instrument called a **sextant**. The measurements tell the navigators their location in the world. By looking at stars millions of light-years away, people can figure out their location on Earth. Amazing!

Did you know?

Animals use stars to navigate, too. Some dung beetles orient themselves using the light from the Milky Way. Just think, even little bugs use the stars to find their way.

19

Chapter 4

Navigation today

Not many people use stars to **navigate** anymore, but they still look to the sky to find their way. Today, most people use GPS, or the Global Positioning System, which is made up of about 30 **satellites orbiting** the planet. People use GPS on land and at sea.

How GPS works

There is a fun game called Marco Polo named after the famous explorer. Have you ever played? It's the game where one person closes his or her eyes and shouts "Marco". Then friends all shout "Polo". The person who has his or her eyes closed can tell where the friends are by listening where their voices are coming from.

Find out more

Research the explorer Marco Polo. Find out when and where he travelled.

GPS works in a similar way to the game Marco Polo. A device called a GPS receiver, like a smartphone, makes contact with at least four GPS satellites. The receiver listens to messages from the satellites, which all have super-precise clocks. By measuring how long the messages take to come from the satellites, the receiver pinpoints its location on the planet.

Don't always depend on technology!

Thanks to GPS, it's easier than ever to find your way. If you make a wrong turn, GPS will tell you where to go.

But GPS isn't perfect, and some people worry that we rely on it too much. Instead of making memory maps, people are just following the GPS. There are stories of people driving into lakes or down park steps because the GPS was wrong and the person using it didn't notice. These mistakes can be deadly.

Think about ...

Think about what would happen if your smartphone battery died and you couldn't use GPS. How would you find your way? Make a list of other things you could use to find your way.

Conclusion

So, even as technology has changed, it's still important to pay attention. Know where you are. Think about where you are going. Understand how to get where you are going. Keep making memory maps. That's how you will find your way.

Glossary

Grandma's house

convenient easy

hull the bottom section of a boat or ship

intricate having many detailed and complex parts

landmarks objects on land that can be seen easily from a distance

navigate to find a way to get to a place, especially through the open seas

Northern Hemisphere the half of the earth that is above (north of) the equator, or midline

oral history stories and information from the past as told by people from their experiences

orbiting moving around a star or planet in a set path

peninsula a piece of land attached to a larger piece of land that is almost totally surrounded by water

reefs long lines of rocks or coral found just under the water in an ocean

route the path taken to get from one place to another

satellites moons or spacecraft that orbit a planet

seafaring using the sea to travel on

sextant a navigational instrument used to measure the height of the sun above the horizon

Southern Hemispere the half of the earth that is below (south of) the equator, or midline

star compass a map made by Polynesian people using the stars, that allows them to know where they are when travelling at sea

stationary not moving, fixed in one place

vast very large in size

visualise to form an image or picture in your mind

Index